TEAM SPIRIT ®

SMART BOOKS FOR YOUNG FANS

THE SAN DIEGO PADRES

BY
MARK STEWART

New Hanover County Public Library
201 Chestnut Street
Wilmington, North Carolina 28401

NORWOOD HOUSE PRESS
CHICAGO, ILLINOIS

Norwood House Press
P.O. Box 316598
Chicago, Illinois 60631

For information regarding Norwood House Press, please visit our website at:
www.norwoodhousepress.com or call 866-565-2900.

All photos courtesy of Getty Images except the following:
Topps, Inc. (6, 7, 15, 28, 30, 34 all, 35 top left & right, 36, 41, 42 bottom left),
Tom DiPace (4, 11, 14, 29, 33, 35 bottom, 37, 38), Black Book Partners Archives (22, 31, 40),
Continental Baking Company (42 top left), San Diego Padres (43 left),
Author's Collection (45), Matt Richman (48).
Cover Photo: Andy Hayt/Getty Images

The memorabilia and artifacts pictured in this book are presented for educational and informational purposes,
and come from the collection of the author.

Editor: Mike Kennedy
Designer: Ron Jaffe
Project Management: Black Book Partners, LLC.
Special thanks to Topps, Inc.

Library of Congress Cataloging-in-Publication Data

Stewart, Mark, 1960-
   The San Diego Padres / by Mark Stewart. -- Library ed.
      p. cm. -- (Team spirit)
   Includes bibliographical references and index.
   Summary: "A Team Spirit Baseball edition featuring the San Diego Padres
that chronicles the history and accomplishments of the team. Includes access
to the Team Spirit website, which provides additional information, updates
and photos"--Provided by publisher.
   ISBN 978-1-59953-495-4 (library : alk. paper) -- ISBN 978-1-60357-375-7
(ebook) 1. San Diego Padres (Baseball team : National League of
Professional Baseball Clubs)--History--Juvenile literature. I. Title.
   GV875.S33G663 2012
   796.357'6409794985--dc23
                                        2011048205

Manufactured in the United States of America in North Mankato, Minnesota.
196N—012012

COVER PHOTO: The Padres get excited in the dugout after a home run.

TABLE OF CONTENTS

ABOUT OUR GLOSSARY

In this book, there may be several words that you are reading for the first time. Some are sports words, some are new vocabulary words, and some are familiar words that are used in an unusual way. All of these words are defined on page 46. Throughout the book, sports words appear in **bold type**. Regular vocabulary words appear in ***bold italic type***.

MEET THE PADRES

The baseball season lasts more than six months. A lot can happen during that time. Some teams race into the lead, while others wait until the final month before making an amazing charge to the top. The San Diego Padres have won both ways. They are full of surprises.

Even when the Padres don't finish in first place, they usually give their fans plenty of thrills. The players are always searching for an edge that will help them win. They play smart, exciting baseball. They play hard until the final out of every game.

This book tells the story of the Padres. San Diego is a great place to live and work. It is a warm and friendly city where different *cultures* blend together. You can see it in the stands at a baseball game, and you can also see it in the San Diego locker room. Few teams in baseball—or any other sport—represent their city as well as the Padres do.

Manager Bud Black gives his players advice during a 2010 game.

GLORY DAYS

During the 20th century, Southern California became a baseball hotbed. Good weather and a growing population meant the game could be played all year long. In 1958, the Dodgers moved from Brooklyn to Los Angeles. Three years later, the Angels began play in Southern California. In 1969, the **National League (NL)** added two new teams. California's southernmost city, San Diego, was chosen for one of these teams. The Padres were born.

SAN DIEGO OUTFIELD

CLARENCE GASTON PADRES

The team's owner was a banker named C. Arnholt Smith. He had previously owned a club in the **minor leagues**. It was also called the San Diego Padres. Smith saw no reason to change the name of his new team in the **major leagues**.

Building a winner posed a greater challenge. The Padres tried to find

LEFT: Clarence "Cito" Gaston
RIGHT: Dave Winfield

players that other teams had overlooked. They discovered some good ones in Nate Colbert, Cito Gaston, Clay Kirby, Dave Roberts, and Ollie Brown. Unfortunately, they still finished last in the **NL West** year after year.

In 1974, Smith had to sell the Padres after his bank failed. He found a buyer in Ray Kroc, who had built the McDonald's fast-food empire. Kroc was used to giving orders and getting results. He was not used to losing.

Kroc needed great patience to make it through his first 10 seasons as owner of the Padres. The team had only one winning year during that time. For Kroc and San Diego fans, exciting players such as Dave Winfield, Gene Richards, Ozzie Smith, and Rollie Fingers made the losing a little easier.

The Padres finally began to play winning baseball in the early 1980s. The team put it all together in 1984. Young outfielders Tony

Gwynn and Kevin McReynolds led a club that included *veterans* Steve Garvey, Graig Nettles, Garry Templeton, and Goose Gossage. Manager Dick Williams made all the right moves, and the Padres won the **pennant**.

San Diego fans had to wait 14 years for the team's next trip to the **World Series**. During that time, a lot of good players came and went. Stars who wore the Padres uniform included John Kruk, Benito Santiago, Bip Roberts, Tony Fernandez, Roberto Alomar, Gary Sheffield, Fred McGriff, Bruce Hurst, and Andy Benes. None of those players could lead the team back to the World Series.

Finally, in 1998, San Diego reached the top again. Gwynn was the leader of a club that starred

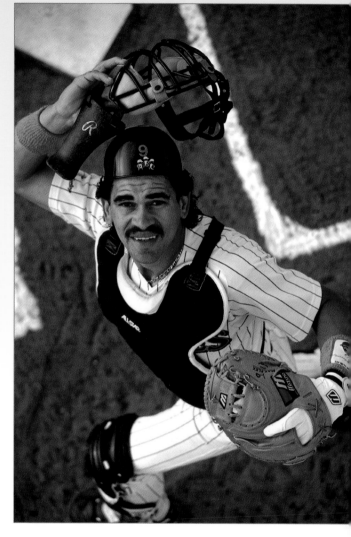

pitchers Kevin Brown and Trevor Hoffman. Sluggers Ken Caminiti and Greg Vaughn provided power at the plate. Bruce Bochy was

LEFT: Tony Gwynn batted over .350 seven times for the Padres.
ABOVE: Benito Santiago was the top catcher in the NL when he played in San Diego.

one of the best managers in baseball. It was an exciting season for San Diego, but it ended with a loss to the New York Yankees in the World Series. The Padres entered the 21st century still searching for their first championship.

In 2004, the Padres moved into a new stadium. It favored teams with good pitching, speed, and defense. San Diego found a winning formula by mixing older players with promising young stars. Hoffman, Brian Giles, and Greg Maddux provided great leadership. Hoffman made the biggest headlines. When he retired, he held the all-time record for **saves**.

Meanwhile, players such as Adrian Gonzalez, Khalil Greene, Jake Peavy, and Heath Bell learned how to succeed in the majors. Opponents knew they were in for a battle whenever they faced the Padres. San Diego returned to the **playoffs** in 2005 and 2006. The team missed the **postseason** by one victory in 2007.

During the seasons that followed, San Diego decided to rebuild its club around young talent. Although they lacked experience, the Padres played hard and nearly won the NL West again in 2010. They continued to bring new players into the lineup, including Cameron Maybin, Chase Headley, Anthony Rizzo, Kyle Blanks, and Edinson Volquez. The Padres are counting on a new core of young stars to help them return to the World Series.

LEFT: The Padres lift Trevor Hoffman onto their shoulders after his 500th save.
ABOVE: Heath Bell fires a pitch. He followed in Hoffman's footsteps.

HOME TURF

From 1969 to 2003, the Padres played in San Diego Stadium. In 1980, it was renamed Jack Murphy Stadium. Murphy was a sportswriter who helped bring big-league baseball to San Diego.

In 2004, the Padres moved into a beautiful new ballpark. It is one of the most *scenic* in the country. From the stands, fans can see San Diego Bay, the downtown skyline, Balboa Park, and the mountains that border the city.

Another eye-catching feature at the Padres' park is the Western Metal Supply Company Building. You can't miss it. The building is located down the left field line! It houses the Padres' team store, rooms for parties, and a restaurant with all kinds of delicious food, including sushi.

BY THE NUMBERS

- The Padres' stadium has 42,691 seats.
- The distance from home plate to the left field foul pole is 336 feet.
- The distance from home plate to the center field fence is 396 feet.
- The distance from home plate to the right field foul pole is 322 feet.

The St. Louis Cardinals and Padres line up before a 2006 playoff game.

DRESSED FOR SUCCESS

From 1969 to 1991, the main colors of the Padres were brown and gold. Their caps had the city's initials, *SD*. San Diego borrowed its cap and colors from the city's minor-league team, which had also been called the Padres.

During the 1970s, the Padres changed their uniform almost every year. From 1972 to 1974, the players often wore bright gold from head to toe. During the 1990s, the Padres began using new colors, including navy blue. Today, the team will even take the field in camouflage uniforms.

For many years, San Diego's *logo* showed a friar swinging a bat. A friar is a type of religious leader. Spanish-speaking friars—often called "Padres" by the people they served—were among the first Europeans to settle the southern part of California. Since the 1990s, the Padres have used a logo that shows a wave from the Pacific Ocean. San Diego is one of America's most beautiful seaside cities.

LEFT: Mat Latos wears the team's road uniform during a 2011 game.
ABOVE: Randy Jones models the San Diego uniform from the late 1970s.

WE WON!

When the Padres opened their new stadium in 2004, two National League pennants were raised over the stands. The first belonged to the 1984 team. That club reached the World Series with a lineup built by Jack McKeon and managed by Dick Williams.

McKeon traded for Garry Templeton, Ed Whitson, and Graig Nettles. He also signed **free agents** Steve Garvey and Goose Gossage. These stars joined Tony Gwynn, Alan Wiggins, Kevin McReynolds, Eric Show, and Mark Thurmond. Under Williams, San Diego won the NL West by 12 games.

The Padres faced the Chicago Cubs in the **National League Championship Series (NLCS)**. Back then, the NLCS was a best-of-five series. The Cubs won the first two games, but San Diego did not give up. In Game 3, Whitson pitched very well, and McReynolds hit a three-run homer for a 7–1 victory. In the next game, Garvey slammed a home run in the ninth inning to beat the Cubs 7–5.

Game 5 would decide the NL pennant. It started badly for the Padres when they fell behind by three runs. Williams went to his **bullpen**, and San Diego held the Cubs scoreless the rest of the day. Meanwhile, the Padres fought back with their bats. Gwynn delivered the key hit in the seventh inning to give his team the lead. Gossage got the final six outs, and the Padres completed an amazing comeback for a 6–3 victory. They were league champions for the first time!

The Padres met the Detroit Tigers in the 1984 World Series. They got a lot of hits, but not when they needed them most. The two teams played five very close games. Unfortunately, San Diego won only one.

LEFT: Goose Gossage was one of the free agents who helped the Padres win their first pennant.   **ABOVE**: Tony Gwynn led the team to the World Series in 1984 and 1998.

The Padres team that took the 1998 pennant also starred Gwynn. He was the top hitter in a lineup that included sluggers Greg Vaughn and Ken Caminiti. However, the key for the Padres was great pitching. Kevin Brown and Andy Ashby were two of the best starters in the NL, and Trevor Hoffman led the league with 53 saves. Manager Bruce Bochy handled the staff perfectly all year long.

In the opening round of the playoffs, the Padres defeated the Houston Astros. Brown's pitching made the difference. San Diego also benefited from

three home runs by Jim Leyritz, the team's backup catcher. The Padres next faced the Atlanta Braves in the NLCS.

The Braves were expected to win because of their excellent pitching. The Padres surprised Atlanta in Game 1 when Caminiti hit a 10th-inning home run to produce a victory. San Diego then turned to its secret weapon. His name was Sterling Hitchcock, and the Braves could score only one run against him. The young left-hander won Game 3 and Game 6. The Padres were NL champions again, and Hitchcock was voted the series **Most Valuable Player (MVP)**.

Hitchcock also pitched well against the Yankees in the World Series, but the Padres could not hold back New York's hitters. San Diego fans would have to wait for the team's first championship.

LEFT: Jim Leyritz rounds the bases after a home run in the 1998 playoffs.
ABOVE: Sterling Hitchcock delivers a pitch in Game 6 of the 1998 NLCS.

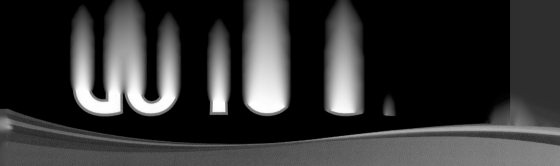

To be a true star in baseball, you need more than a quick bat and a strong arm. You have to be a "go-to guy"—someone the manager wants on the pitcher's mound or in the batter's box when it matters most. Fans of the Padres have had a lot to cheer about over the years, including these great stars …

THE PIONEERS

NATE COLBERT   First Baseman

• BORN: 4/9/1946   • PLAYED FOR TEAM: 1969 TO 1974

The Padres plucked powerful Nate Colbert off the roster of the Houston Astros before the 1969 season. He became San Diego's first star. In 1972, the team scored only 488 runs. Colbert drove in 111 of them.

DAVE WINFIELD   Outfielder

• BORN: 10/3/1951   • PLAYED FOR TEAM: 1973 TO 1980

When Dave Winfield joined the Padres, he was not sure whether he would be a pitcher or an outfielder. He had starred at both positions in college. Winfield went on to win two **Gold Gloves** in the outfield and was named an **All-Star** four times.

RANDY JONES   Pitcher

- BORN: 1/12/1950   • PLAYED FOR TEAM: 1973 TO 1980

Randy Jones hurt his arm and lost 22 games for the Padres in 1974. A year later, he perfected a slow, sinking pitch and became the league's best starter. Jones led the NL with a 2.24 **earned run average (ERA)** in 1975 and won the **Cy Young Award** in 1976.

ROLLIE FINGERS   Pitcher

- BORN: 8/25/1946

- PLAYED FOR TEAM: 1977 TO 1980

The four years that Rollie Fingers pitched for the Padres were four of his best. He led the NL in saves twice and was the league's top relief pitcher in 1977, 1978, and 1980.

OZZIE SMITH   Shortstop

- BORN: 12/26/1954

- PLAYED FOR TEAM: 1978 TO 1981

Ten games into his **rookie** season, Ozzie Smith made a bare-handed fielding play that many fans think was the greatest ever. That same season, he started his most famous move. On Fan Appreciation Day, Smith did a mid-air flip on the way to his position in the first inning.

RIGHT: Rollie Fingers

TONY GWYNN   Outfielder

• BORN: 5/9/1960   • PLAYED FOR TEAM: 1982 TO 2001

Tony Gwynn could do everything on a baseball field. He won eight batting championships and five Gold Gloves, and led the Padres to the World Series twice. Gwynn nearly hit .400 one year. He finished his career with a .338 average and more than 3,000 hits. Gwynn entered the **Hall of Fame** in 2007.

TREVOR HOFFMAN   Pitcher

• BORN: 10/13/1967   • PLAYED FOR TEAM: 1993 TO 2008

Trevor Hoffman started his career as an infielder but switched to pitching in 1991. He used a good fastball and a great **change-up** to keep hitters guessing for years and years. In 2007, he became the first reliever to reach 500 saves.

KEN CAMINITI   Third Baseman

• BORN: 4/21/1963   • DIED: 10/10/2004
• PLAYED FOR TEAM: 1995 TO 1998

Ken Caminiti was known as a good fielder, hitter, and team leader when he played for the Houston Astros. No one knew just how good until he joined the Padres. Caminiti smashed 40 homers and won a Gold Glove in 1996. In 1998, he helped the Padres win the pennant.

JAKE PEAVY   Pitcher

- BORN: 5/31/1981
- PLAYED FOR TEAM: 2002 TO 2009

When the Padres brought Jake Peavy to the big leagues, they expected big things. He did not disappoint them. He led the NL in ERA in 2004 and in strikeouts in 2005. In a 2007 game, Peavy struck out nine batters in a row. He won the NL Cy Young Award that season, too.

ADRIAN GONZALEZ   First Baseman

- BORN: 5/8/1982
- PLAYED FOR TEAM: 2006 TO 2010

Adrian Gonzalez was the top pick in the 2000 **draft**. He struggled with two other teams before the Padres gave him a chance. Gonzalez proved to be one of the best hitters and fielders in the league.

MAT LATOS   Pitcher

- BORN: 12/9/1987   • PLAYED FOR TEAM: 2009 TO 2011

When Mat Latos was pitching in the minor leagues, many baseball scouts said he would one day be a star. He had a powerful fastball and a change-up that kept hitters off-balance. Latos proved the scouts right when he pitched a one-hitter in his second season with San Diego.

LEFT: Ken Caminiti
RIGHT: Jake Peavy

Early in their history, the Padres didn't look far for managers. The Los Angeles Dodgers had a lot of smart people running their team. San Diego often tapped into this resource. Padres managers Preston Gomez, Don Zimmer, Roger Craig, Frank Howard, and

Dick Williams had all been Dodgers in the past.

Williams was the manager who led the Padres to their first pennant, in 1984. He demanded extra effort from his players at all times. The Padres listened to Williams because he had already won pennants with two other teams.

San Diego's next pennant came in 1998. Bruce Bochy was the manager that year. Bochy had been a catcher for Williams on the 1984 team. He was the first Padres player to become the team's

LEFT: Dick Williams watches his team in 1984.
RIGHT: Bruce Bochy takes a trip to the mound in 2006.

manager. Bochy had been hired to manage in 1995. One season later, he led the Padres to first place in the NL West and was named Manager of the Year. Two years later, the Padres made it all the way to the World Series.

In all, Bochy managed the team for 12 seasons. During that time, San Diego won four NL West crowns. Padres fans knew Bochy was a smart leader, but sometimes they complained that he had a dull personality. They didn't realize how funny Bochy was in the locker room. He knew how to make his players laugh and keep them relaxed during a long, pressure-packed season.

ONE GREAT DAY

Steve Garvey was one of baseball's best hitters during the 1970s. Age and injuries slowed him down in the 1980s, but the Padres believed he was still a valuable player. When they had a chance to get him, they moved quickly to sign him. Garvey joined the team in 1983 and became a great leader. In 1984, the Padres won the NL West for the first time.

That year, the Padres played the Chicago Cubs in the NLCS. The first team to win three games would win the pennant. San Diego fans were heartbroken when their team lost the first two games, both in Chicago. The Padres came home and won Game 3.

Game 4 was a seesaw battle that was tied 5–5 in the bottom of the ninth inning.

With one out and a runner on first base, Garvey stepped into the batter's box against Lee Smith, Chicago's overpowering relief pitcher. Garvey had already played a great game. He had three hits and had driven home three runs. Smith fired a fastball, and Garvey launched a long fly to center field. The ball cleared the fence for the game-winning home run.

The fans went crazy as Garvey circled the bases. The series was now tied at two games each. The next day, San Diego won 6–3 to capture its first NL crown. Garvey drove home another run in that game and was named the series MVP.

LEFT: Steve Garvey takes a cut during the 1984 NLCS.
ABOVE: Garvey celebrates his game-winning home run in Game 4.

LEGEND HAS IT

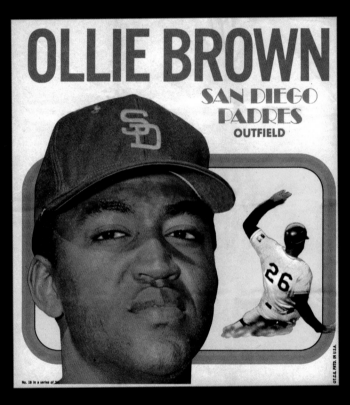

WHO HAD THE BEST ARM IN TEAM HISTORY?

LEGEND HAS IT that Ollie Brown did. Brown was the very first Padre. He was the team's top pick in a special player draft held after the 1968 season. Brown played the outfield from 1969 to 1972. During warm-ups, he would give the crowd a thrill by throwing the ball from deep right field all the way to third base! Most fans did not know that he had been a pitcher in the minor leagues—and once threw a no-hitter.

ABOVE: Ollie Brown is shown as a baserunner in this 1970 poster.
RIGHT: Mat Latos

28

LEGEND HAS IT that Steve Arlin did. From June 18 to July 18 in 1972, he pitched two one-hitters and three two-hitters. Unfortunately, the Padres did not have much hitting that season. Arlin won just three of the five games.

WHO WAS THE PADRES' STREAKIEST PITCHER?

LEGEND HAS IT that Mat Latos was. In 2010, Latos went 15 starts in a row without giving up more than two earned runs. It was the longest such streak in more than 100 years. Latos put together another streak that wasn't as much fun for him. He lost his last five starts in 2010 and began the 2011 season by losing five more games. He finally got a win to end a 10-game losing streak!

People who trade baseball cards love to swap one All-Star player for another. In real life, this almost never happens. Usually, the team trading the star is looking for young talent in return—or perhaps two or three lesser players to "plug holes" in its lineup. That is why San Diego fans were in shock on December 5, 1990. On that day, they learned that Roberto Alomar and Joe Carter had been traded to the Toronto Blue Jays for Fred McGriff and Tony Fernandez. It was one of the biggest trades of talent in history.

All four players were All-Stars. Alomar was the most exciting young second baseman in the NL. Carter had just set a new team record with 115 **runs batted in (RBIs)**. One year earlier, the Padres had traded Roberto's brother, Sandy, to get Carter. Now both Alomars were gone. Fernandez was the finest shortstop in baseball. He had won four Gold Gloves for his excellent fielding and led the AL with 17 triples

in 1990. McGriff was a power-hitting first baseman. He had topped the AL in homers in 1989.

How did the trade work out? Toronto fans were very happy with the results. Alomar and Carter helped the Blue Jays win the World Series in 1992 and 1993. Alomar would go on to earn 10 Gold Gloves and become a Hall of Famer.

The Padres did not win a World Series with McGriff and Fernandez, but both players did well in San Diego. McGriff became the team's first home run champion in 1992. That year, he launched 35 long balls. Fernandez was an All-Star for San Diego in 1992. Still, if the Padres could do it all over again, their fans would probably say *No Deal!*

TEAM SPIRIT

A ticket to a Padres game is like an invitation to a party with family and friends. It has been that way for *generations*. The star of that party is often Jerry Coleman, the team's announcer. Lots of fans listen to Coleman on the radio while they are in the stadium. In 2011, he celebrated his 40th year calling games.

The Padres are also known for their mascots. In the 1970s, the San Diego Chicken became baseball's most famous mascot. He was the first to jump on the field and have fun with players and umpires. The Chicken worked for a radio station, so officially he was never the Padres' mascot. That honor went to the

Swinging Friar, a large-than-life "padre." On Sundays, he dresses in a special camouflage robe to honor fans who are serving in the military.

LEFT: The Swinging Friar gets fans into the game.
ABOVE: San Diego's famous Chicken dives into third base.

TIMELINE

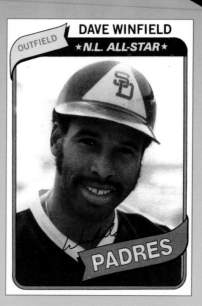

Dave
Winfield

1974
The team is
purchased by
Ray Kroc.

1979
Dave Winfield
wins the team's
first Gold Glove.

1969
The Padres play
their first season.

1984
The Padres win their
first NL pennant.

1992
Gary Sheffield leads the
NL with a .330 average.

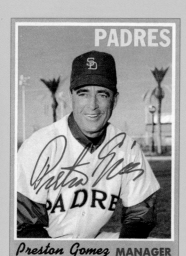

Preston Gomez
was the team's
manager in 1969.

Gary
Sheffield

Heath
Bell

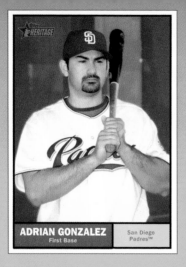

Adrian
Gonzalez

1996
Ken Caminiti wins
the MVP award.

2007
Trevor Hoffman
saves his 500th game.

2010
Adrian Gonzalez is an All-Star
for the third year in a row.

1997
Tony Gwynn wins
his eighth batting title.

1998
The Padres win
their second pennant.

2011
Heath Bell ties Trevor Hoffman's
team record of 41 saves in a row.

Tony
Gwynn

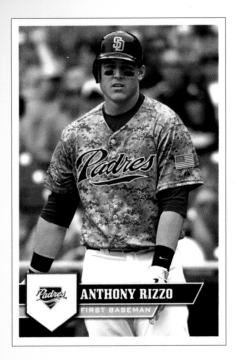

ANTHONY RIZZO
FIRST BASEMAN

Comeback Kid

When Anthony Rizzo played his first big-league game for the Padres in 2011, it was truly a time to celebrate. Three years earlier, Rizzo had overcome Hodgkin's lymphoma, a form of cancer.

Nate the Great

In 1972, Nate Colbert had a day to remember. He hit two singles and two homers in the first game of a doubleheader against the Atlanta Braves. He added three more homers in the second game. In all, he drove in 13 runs.

Streaking!

Benito Santiago holds the team record for the longest hitting streak. In 1987, the catcher got a hit in 34 games in a row.

ABOVE: Anthony Rizzo   **RIGHT**: Adrian Gonzalez

ADRIAN GOES GONZO

In a 2009 game against the Milwaukee Brewers, Adrian Gonzalez went 6–for–6. He was the first Padre to get six hits in a nine-inning game.

STAYING PUT

In 1974, the Padres nearly moved to Washington, D.C. They would have been named the Nationals. Instead, Ray Kroc bought the Padres and kept them in San Diego.

DON'T WE KNOW YOU?

In 1971, the Padres traded their best pitcher, Dave Roberts, to the Houston Astros. A few months later the team signed a power-hitting third baseman. His name was also Dave Roberts.

SPEED DEMONS

In 1980, Gene Richards, Ozzie Smith, and Jerry Mumphrey each stole more than 50 bases. It was the first time in history three teammates had done this.

TALKING BASEBALL

"He was one of the best players I ever saw, and he was probably the smartest and most dedicated."

▶ **BRUCE BOCHY**, ON TONY GWYNN

"If you work hard, good things will happen."

▶ **TONY GWYNN**, REMEMBERING THE BEST ADVICE HE GOT FROM HIS FATHER

"The fans are really what matters. They're the ones that show up. They're the ones who pay our salary."

▶ **HEATH BELL**, ON WHY HE ALWAYS GIVES HIS BEST WHEN HE TAKES THE MOUND

ABOVE: Bruce Bochy
RIGHT: Team owner Ray Kroc talks to manager John McNamara.

"Luck is a *dividend* of sweat. The more you sweat, the luckier you get."

▶ **RAY KROC**, *ON THE VALUE OF HARD WORK*

"To me baseball is the best game of all."

▶ **DAVE WINFIELD**, *ON WHY HE CHOSE BASEBALL OVER FOOTBALL AND BASKETBALL*

"I went at the game 100 percent. I got the most out of what I was given."

▶ **TREVOR HOFFMAN**, *ON WHAT MADE HIM ONE OF BASEBALL'S GREATEST RELIEF PITCHERS*

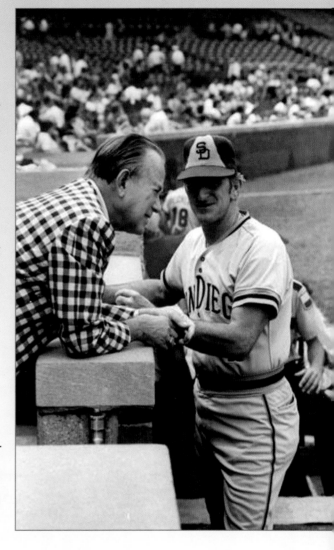

"It was pure, it was crisp. It was the biggest hit in this franchise's history."

▶ **TONY GWYNN**, *ON STEVE GARVEY'S HOME RUN IN GAME 4 OF THE 1984 NLCS*

GREAT DEBATES

People who root for the Padres love to compare their favorite moments, teams, and players. Some debates have been going on for years! How would you settle these classic baseball arguments?

THE 1984 PADRES WOULD BEAT THE 1998 PADRES IN A SERIES ...

... because they had experienced stars who knew what it took to win a pennant. Steve Garvey, Graig Nettles, and Goose Gossage were all-time greats. Terry Kennedy was one of the best catchers in baseball. The greater the pressure, the better the Padres played. Also, San Diego had a 24-year-old batting champ named Tony Gwynn. Maybe you've heard of him?

WAIT A MINUTE. THE 1998 PADRES WOULD WIN THAT SERIES EASILY ...

... because they had Gwynn (LEFT)—the most experienced player of all! In 1984, he was young and still learning about life in the majors. By 1998, he had eight batting titles under his belt. Gwynn was also surrounded by veterans such as Ken Caminiti, Steve Finley, Greg Vaughn, and Kevin Brown. They made the 1998 Padres tough to beat.

RANDY JONES HAD THE GREATEST YEAR OF ANY SAN DIEGO PITCHER ...

... because he set a team record with 22 wins in 1976. That season, Jones (RIGHT) not only led the NL in victories, he also pitched the most innings in the league. He started 40 games and finished 25 of them. Jones was the starter in the All-Star Game in July, and at the end of the year he won the Cy Young Award. That's not bad for a pitcher who played for a fifth-place team.

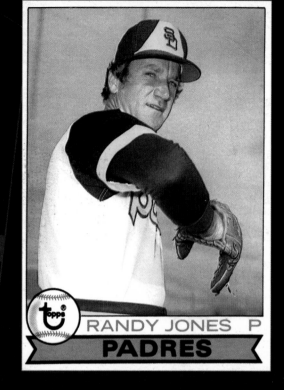

RANDY JONES   P
PADRES

NOT BAD. BUT NOT BETTER THAN TREVOR HOFFMAN'S BEST YEAR ...

... because in 1998 he set a team record of his own with 53 saves. Hoffman was the best relief pitcher in the NL that season. In 73 innings, he struck out 86 batters and gave up just 41 hits. He added three more saves in the playoffs. Of course, Hoffman was just getting started at that point. He would go on to save more than 550 games for the Padres in his career.

The great Padres teams and players have left their marks on the record books. These are the "best of the best" …

PADRES AWARD WINNERS

WINNER	AWARD	YEAR
Randy Jones	Comeback Player of the Year	1975
Randy Jones	Cy Young Award	1976
Butch Metzger	Rookie of the Year*	1976
Gaylord Perry	Cy Young Award	1978
Steve Garvey	NLCS MVP	1984
LaMarr Hoyt	All-Star Game MVP	1985
Benito Santiago	Rookie of the Year	1987
Mark Davis	Cy Young Award	1989
Gary Sheffield	Comeback Player of the Year	1992
Bruce Bochy	Manager of the Year	1996
Ken Caminiti	Most Valuable Player	1996
Greg Vaughn	Comeback Player of the Year	1998
Sterling Hitchcock	NLCS MVP	1998
Jake Peavy	Cy Young Award	2007

The annual award given to each league's best first-year player.

GAYLORD PERRY
SAN DIEGO PADRES p

Gaylord Perry

Mark Davis

Gary Sheffield

PADRES ACHIEVEMENTS

ACHIEVEMENT	YEAR
NL West Champions	1984
NL Pennant Winners	1984
NL West Champions	1996
NL West Champions	1998
NL Pennant Winners	1998
NL West Champions	2005
NL West Champions	2006

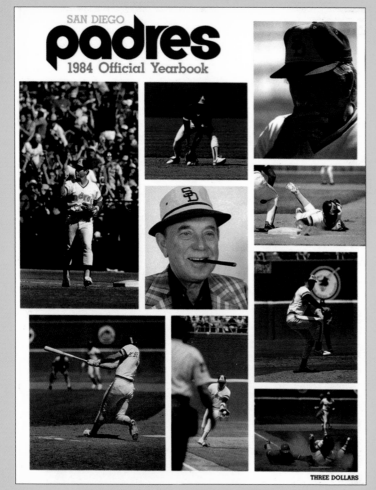

ABOVE: Brian Giles was the team's top hitter in 2005.
LEFT: The 1984 yearbook shows owner Ray Kroc in the middle. Kroc passed away early that year and did not get to see his team win the pennant.

PINPOINTS

The history of a baseball team is made up of many smaller stories. These stories take place all over the map—not just in the city a team calls "home." Match the pushpins on these maps to the **TEAM FACTS**, and you will begin to see the story of the Padres unfold!

1 San Diego, California—*The Padres have played here since 1969.*

2 Los Angeles, California—*Tony Gwynn was born here.*

3 Atlanta, Georgia—*The Padres won the 1998 pennant here.*

4 Colorado Springs, Colorado—*Goose Gossage was born here.*

5 St. Paul, Minnesota—*Dave Winfield was born here.*

6 Steubenville, Ohio—*Rollie Fingers was born here.*

7 Detroit, Michigan—*The Padres faced the Tigers in the 1984 World Series here.*

8 St. Louis, Missouri—*Nate Colbert was born here.*

9 Tuscaloosa, Alabama—*Ollie Brown was born here.*

10 Central Preston, Cuba—*Preston Gomez was born here.*

11 Ponce, Puerto Rico—*Benito Santiago was born here.*

12 Landes de Bussac, France—*Bruce Bochy was born here.*

Nate Colbert

GLOSSARY

🧢 **BASEBALL WORDS**
🧠 **VOCABULARY WORDS**

🧢 **ALL-STAR**—A player who is selected to play in baseball's annual All-Star Game.

🧢 **BULLPEN**—The area where a team's relief pitchers warm up. This word also describes the group of relief pitchers in this area.

🧢 **CHANGE-UP**—A slow pitch disguised to look like a fastball.

🧠 *CULTURES*—The beliefs, customs, and way of living shared by large groups of people.

🧢 **CY YOUNG AWARD**—The award given each year to each league's best pitcher.

🧠 *DIVIDEND*—A benefit from an idea or action.

🧢 **DRAFT**—The annual meeting at which teams take turns choosing the best players in high school and college.

🧢 **EARNED RUN AVERAGE (ERA)**—A statistic that measures how many runs a pitcher gives up for every nine innings he pitches.

🧢 **FREE AGENTS**—Players who are allowed to join any team that wants them.

🧠 *GENERATIONS*—Periods of years roughly equal to the time it takes for a person to be born, grow up, and have children.

🧢 **GOLD GLOVES**—The awards given each year to baseball's best fielders.

🧢 **HALL OF FAME**—The museum in Cooperstown, New York, where baseball's greatest players are honored.

🧠 *LOGO*—A symbol or design that represents a company or team.

🧢 **MAJOR LEAGUES**—The top level of professional baseball.

🧢 **MINOR LEAGUES**—The many professional leagues that help develop players for the major leagues.

🧢 **MOST VALUABLE PLAYER (MVP)**—The award given each year to each league's top player; an MVP is also selected for the World Series and the All-Star Game.

🧢 **NATIONAL LEAGUE (NL)**—The older of the two major leagues; the NL began play in 1876.

🧢 **NATIONAL LEAGUE CHAMPIONSHIP SERIES (NLCS)**—The playoff series that has decided the NL pennant since 1969.

🧢 **NL WEST**—A group of National League teams that play in the western part of the country.

🧢 **PENNANT**—A league championship. The term comes from the triangular flag awarded to each season's champion, beginning in the 1870s.

🧢 **PLAYOFFS**—The games played after the regular season to determine which teams will advance to the World Series.

🧢 **POSTSEASON**—The games played after the regular season, including the playoffs and World Series.

🧢 **ROOKIE**—A player in his first season.

🧢 **RUNS BATTED IN (RBIs)**—A statistic that counts the number of runners a batter drives home.

🧢 **SAVES**—A statistic that counts the number of times a relief pitcher finishes off a close victory for his team.

🧠 *SCENIC*—Offering beautiful natural views.

🧠 *VETERANS*—Players who have great experience.

🧢 **WORLD SERIES**—The world championship series played between the American League and National League pennant winners.

EXTRA INNINGS

TEAM SPIRIT introduces a great way to stay up to date with your team! Visit our **EXTRA INNINGS** link and get connected to the latest and greatest updates. **EXTRA INNINGS** serves as a young reader's ticket to an exclusive web page—with more stories, fun facts, team records, and photos of the Padres. Content is updated during and after each season. The **EXTRA INNINGS** feature also enables readers to send comments and letters to the author! Log onto:

www.norwoodhousepress.com/library.aspx

and click on the tab: **TEAM SPIRIT** to access **EXTRA INNINGS**.

Read all the books in the series to learn more about professional sports. For a complete listing of the baseball, basketball, football, and hockey teams in the **TEAM SPIRIT** series, visit our website at:

www.norwoodhousepress.com/library.aspx

ON THE ROAD

SAN DIEGO PADRES
100 Park Boulevard
San Diego, California 92101
(619) 795-5000
sandiego.padres.mlb.com

NATIONAL BASEBALL HALL OF FAME AND MUSEUM
25 Main Street
Cooperstown, New York 13326
(888) 425-5633
www.baseballhalloffame.org

ON THE BOOKSHELF

To learn more about the sport of baseball, look for these books at your library or bookstore:

- Augustyn, Adam (editor). *The Britannica Guide to Baseball.* New York, NY: Rosen Publishing, 2011.

- Dreier, David. *Baseball: How It Works.* North Mankato, MN: Capstone Press, 2010.

- Stewart, Mark. *Ultimate 10: Baseball.* New York, NY: Gareth Stevens Publishing, 2009.

INDEX

PAGE NUMBERS IN **BOLD** REFER TO ILLUSTRATIONS.

ABOUT THE AUTHOR

MARK STEWART has written more than 50 books on baseball and over 150 sports books for kids. He grew up in New York City during the 1960s rooting for the Yankees and Mets, and was lucky enough to meet players from both teams. Mark comes from a family of writers. His grandfather was Sunday Editor of *The New York Times,* and his mother was Articles Editor of *Ladies' Home Journal* and *McCall's.* Mark has profiled hundreds of athletes over the past 25 years. He has also written several books about his native New York and New Jersey, his home today. Mark is a graduate of Duke University, with a degree in history. He lives and works in a home overlooking Sandy Hook, New Jersey. You can contact Mark through the Norwood House Press website.